D1606116

THE

art

IN KNOWING ME

poems by

danielle p williams

Florencia,

Because of you, I have decided to live in my truth. To smile when levees tumble and tears roar. To look at life with fresh eyes and understanding. To sit back, breathe, and marvel in the beauty of the legacy you left with me. Because of you, I can reflect on pain and not be broken by it. I can breathe freely, and never be afraid of suffocation. I can draw strength from the remnants of your laugh, and live life without restriction, or reserve. Because of you, I can love freely without an ounce of fear.

This is for you.

evolution.

I am made of cinnamon, gold, and God. My roots are home grown. They are given light from the sun of the Motherland and drenched in the blue water waves of the Marianas. They have sprouted into tousled curls that spend fifty percent of their existence in tangles. Into attitude and back talk. Into sarcasm and awkwardness. Into curiosity. Into challenge. Into an abundance of knowledge, and thinking you have all of the answers. Into laughs that marinate in the ears of loved ones. Into being trapped in moments that are too perfectly complicated to put to words.

I am made of stories and alliteration. I have taken rubble and repurposed righteousness, and hung a gallery full of artwork dedicated to my insecurities. I have garnished canvases with images of love and heartbreak, and splash in rhyme and meter to make it more approachable. I have colored in scars with acrylic paint. Marked my battle wounds with shades of periwinkle and poems written in pain. I take pride in the gut wrenching truth I display amongst the masses. I forget all of the tears that tore past my eyelids as dreams turned into nightmares, and label my failures as an encyclopedia of remembered laughter. I remember that after the worst is over, there is light and I continue to look for the sparkle in my mirror cracked smile.

I am made of the people that came before me. I am his story, and her story, and all of the hardships that brought me to this precise moment. I am potential. I am promise. I am the premise to a body of work that has yet to experience my fire. I am me and make no apologies for anyone who wishes to be offended by my presentations of getting to know myself.

in your honor.

Your hands were soft,

your voice smelled like
risen dough, like it was
in progress of something
beautiful.

You were so beautiful –

generations of women after
you are proof of that.

You were a hell of a match
and sat amongst us fallen
claiming us as the future.

You had faith in us even after
you left, and we will always try
our hardest to never let you down.

We will always try our hardest
to remember the
smell of your voice carrying,
always remember,

progress.

disclaimer.

My poetry is not meant to be convenient. It is meant
to emerge you, full body, in truth. To have you questioning
what it ever meant to be on dry land.

June 9th.

I think I love you.

I think I love you.
Or at least, I love
the way your brow
furrows. Fidgets really.
Right there, at the top
of your forehead.

I used to think
you did it in retaliation,
because you hated
the way I rolled my eyes
to any and every
thing you sent my way.

And so, to dissuade me
from the beautiful architect
of your profile, you would
distort and distract me.

But I always still saw you.
In all your glory.

And now, despite your
crinkled canvas of a face,
now, I know it means

you might just love me too.
Or at least, you love

the way I look away
when our eyes meet.
I only do it because I don't
want you to see me examining
the way your cheeks are
elevated to the tip of your
temples when you smile.

It's quite meticulous really,
my staring that is. And I'm
curious in my convictions
of you because I don't think
I've ever met a man who's
laugh lines jump through the
blueprints of their beard
like the way yours does,
And it's crazy, how vividly
I see you.

How I see you, grinning
at me and I'm so damn
fascinated for about four
or five seconds that I've already
forgotten I'm staring at all.
And then, I look away, and

look back at you and that
damn furrow, forming again
and I proceed to roll my eyes,
and look away again, it's
sickening how cyclical it all is.
And then my eyes, they

reach their resting place,
just in time to meet yours,
and then, you look away again,
and then, there I go... five, six,
seven, shit, now ten seconds later,
and I'm still staring. Gazing really.

Because after that third second,
I've realized that I'm looking
at a man who still sees me
when he starts staring
out into the distance.

Who never, not even
for a second, has forgotten
what our eyes have taught
themselves about each other.

And when I look at you
without a word or sound
to form, I have already
formed a novel of ways
to tell you I love you.
And when I'm staring,

I mean really staring,
unapologetic and
unaware of any
awkwardness, I have
already recited
a poem in my head
to the audience of my

choosing, telling them
just how beautiful
I find your eyes.

a haiku for loving me.

Come, swallow me whole.
Sanctify me in your palms,
sing for me a psalm,

and, in my honor,
glorify me on a cross,
lift me up, in love.

Realize, these eyes
Are not nearly the same as
the other sanctions.

Here lies real laws of
love so exalt me and I'll
prove to be worthy.

grateful.

Because of you,
I hope for things
I never before
thought possible
and i can never be
more grateful or more
proud.

after the dust settled.

June 9th came and went.

I sit in the shadows of my
apartment, half laughing,
half crying at the thought of
ever loving you.

I still remember the
sound of my name
flowing from your lips.

I still remember the
tension in my belly
forming when you held me
at 2am on your mother's
living room floor.

It was too dark to make
out your face, but by then
I had already memorized
your make. In the darkness,
I traced the blueprint of you.
There you were, right there,
smiling back at me.

You were laying in the
stillness, staring at the

ceiling with that grin on
your face because

you thought, maybe,
just maybe, I was
the one for you.

But you allowed those
thoughts to linger,
never let it pass your lips
to form a sentence,
instead, sentenced me
to solitary confinement,
where I would never
again be able to lay
or laugh with you.

I don't know why you
decided to distance
your love from me.

But there I was,
ready to give you
all of me, and you—
you were nowhere.

And with nowhere
to go or hide, I cried

in the dark. I cried
in the light too
because I wanted
everyone to see
what you had
done to me.

Wanted everyone to
know that you had
promised me better.

And now, I'm bitter
and more broken
than I've ever been
because of you.

And you, you were never
man enough to take
a peek at the love
I had drawn out for us.
To marvel and awe
at the art I had
repurposed for you.

And I waited. Waited
for you to figure out
you loved me too.

But you never came for me.

And for two months
after you left, I sat and
wrote poems for you.

I am not built for
these civil wars that
keep raiding in my heart.

I seem to have surrendered
everything but the echo
of your laugh and
our last kiss.

Everything else,
I've tucked neatly in the
past. Packed it all away,
marked lost and found.
Let's see if you ever
come back around.

Sometimes there is art in me.
Sometimes there is doubt.
Sometimes I am not strong enough
to sift through the rubble to find
what's beautiful in me anymore.

first-aid.

There are no band-aids
large enough to cover
my scars.

There are not nearly
enough ways for me
to write how I'm not
healing this time.

And it seems as though
I have forgotten what it
felt like not to bleed for you.

Forgotten how to lay all
of my feelings down with
hopes of nurturing hands.

Over the span of years,
you have decided against
catching me.

And once again,
I have unhinged stitches
that I had promised myself
would stay sealed,
seared away any attempts
of re-entry, and lied, saying

I was ready for accepting new
invitations of knowing me.

As a writer, I am complacent. I let silence fill in days where I am content in my life. But when the day comes where unknown fear arises, my fingers will take to pen and fill pages of all of the ways I will be broken when you are gone.

home.

When I got the call, I knew
that the singing of your voice
against my ear was no longer
an option.

I've never before been so
affected by two words.

I figured mom would be off
consoling her own grief
to call me.

When I saw dad's name
flash on my phone I felt
a heat cower over me.

Our conversation was as
brief as words amongst
passing strangers,

Dad: "She's gone."
Me: "Okay."

dial tone

I felt too much.
My knees buckled.

Every eye that caught
mine turned into silent panic.

I remember two hands
close enough to reach
out and catch me.

I was too scared to look
in her eyes but I knew she
felt my thankfulness.

At that point, gravity
no longer suited me.

Nor did comfort.

Nor did voices that were
anyone's but yours.

I felt too much.

I played the image of
crinkles forming from your
skin as you laughed in my head
on a loop.

I touched my hand
and closed my eyes
and pretended it
was your touch.

I tried to smile like
I knew you were smiling
now that you were finally home.

I tried to imagine a life
without your light and sat
in the stillness until sleep
finally settled me.

daily affirmation:

I can stand this.
I can stand this.
I can stand this.

what's kept in boxes.

Boxes
were meant
for unpacking.

Stacking
regret
on top of
neglect.

Forget
what you
put inside
them —
someone
will unpack
them
eventually.

No telling
the damages
when
they're
opened up.

Careful —
make sure
to label them,
handle with care.

four ways to describe the way her hands shake when her words stop.

1. We lay in the bed staring at the ceiling. I can tell she has a story sitting at the top of her lips. So, I wait. And lay there anticipating her truths to form. Her breaths are 3 seconds longer than mine. When I turn and look at her, her eyes are gridlocked upward. As she begins to speak, her voice shakes like a class seven earthquake. As the levels of her voice rise and she starts to reveal her secrets, I cry. I feel as though I have not protected her like a big sister should have. She tells me she hates him. I do not interject until I know she is finished. I do not diminish her relicts of him.

2. I am still— and wondering just how heavy that kind of weight has bared on her tiny shoulders. Wondering, what kind of slate can be cleansed once poison has drenched it at the ripe of four. She is eighteen now. I take the five years that separate us in age and wear it like battle armor.

3. I thought back to when the two of them left us. My father and my sister. Journeying to the island that gave us life. That taught us to dance with stories laced in our palms. Our mother's lands. We had our mother's hands. And in the important moments of life, when it was time to test the waters, our father revealed himself a traitor.
And though his indiscretions were not new to us, you, my love, were in the thick of it. You were turned sick by it. You were left with the secrets he was too careless to lift from your undergrown shoulders. He never knew they'd turn

the art in knowing me

into boulders. And now, now he has a daughter who looks at him and does not see a father in him.

4. When your words stop, we both lay there crying. I grab your hand. Hold it like I should have all of those years ago. I squeeze thirteen years of a sister's love into your palms. And hope that one day you'll dance the stories of your truths into the realizations of our father, the man who should have known to love you better. Until that day comes, I'll still lay with you. And take the weight of mourning heartbreak off of your hands.

begin again.

I'm constantly at
odds with myself.

I never know
whether to place
blame on my thoughts
for acting so aggressively
against my anxiety,
or *you.*

I carry armfuls of
bruises with me
whenever it's time
for me to begin again.

I carry, pathetic
promises of days that
turn into nights that
dream of lifetimes with you.

And I'm constantly at
awe with the fact that
I can keep dreaming of you
when I haven't been able
to sleep since you left.

lineage.

You are my mother's mother.

You are the map traced in my
palms giving nudge to things
I am still afraid of touching.

five little poems for you.

1. Erase the sound of my name from your lips.

Remove the length of inhales, it took for you
to forget me, and exhale all of the
things I did wrong.

Huff and puff and blow away all the
love in your heart that had been paving its
way to me, away.

2. Tell no one my name. Never let it cross your
mind again. Never let it wander on the
sidewalks of your sanity.

Don't go crazy, on my behalf.

Leave that to me.

3. I wrote your name in permanent ink.
I mistakenly, linked your laugh to my
smile, and in its absence my cheeks have
turned against me.

4. In those brief moments where I do not seek your
eyes, I find myself looking at the sky in all its
beauty and comparing the two, though they
were nowhere near equivalent.

5. Sometimes, I whisper remnants of you in the

confines of my mind, only to be reminded that
you chose to erase me, with no cause or warning and
now, every now and again, I scan for your face in the
crowd and wonder if you'll ever come looking for me
like I do in the evening after the hustle and bustle of
trying to forget you settles.

favorite things.

We used to jump on
beds to the rhythm of
Mariah Carey songs.

Used to scream at the top
of our lungs into hair brushes
and ignore all of the
monsters that lived outside
those bedroom walls.

Whenever we did go outside,
we saw dragonflies the size
of fruit bats, ran parallel to
their fluorescent wings, and soaked
in the breeze that fled from the ocean,

We lived in this notion that
nothing could touch us
unless we let it.

We did this to be strong.

We were creative souls, you and I,
and created our own molds, our
own holdings in life.

We were unattended and wild, and
wistful, and wishful, and bashful all at
the same time.

We ran free on an island we
proclaimed as ours.

We were learning what it
meant to live and survive
in a world where our favorite
things, were not things at all,

but people who saw us form
from bed springs and bad
renditions of r&b love ballads.

People, who looked out for us
on days where the only eyes
watching were crafted from
storms meant for demise.

But we were daughters of the
sand, and decided way back when
we'd make our own stories about
how we'd conquer conflict.

About how we'd one day
rule the world.

funeral.

I have never before witnessed
so much pain in one room.

It was difficult.

To see my brother call
out for you the way he did.

To see cousins, and aunts,
and neighbors and church
members and moms and sisters
and me, fathom the fear of a life
without you.

I have never before witnessed
people grasping for their last
memory of you laughing with them.

It was difficult.

an ode to GoldLink.

And after that, we didn't talk.

Before that, we were gold -
linked chained to each other's
ribs. We were a spectrum of new
black love. Dark skinned women
draped in orange. Decadent. Delicate.
And desired. Look for the speckles of
gold dust falling from their hair, remnants
of last night's history story. Of kings and
queens that look like you and me.
I was your Zipporah, your heroine.
And we journeyed to the ends of our
youth with one another.

We were royal, and in love. And hid
from responsibilities, underneath the
palm trees. And when we were tired of
holding each other we would watch the
sun dance on my ankles as it set. But with
the night came regret. And reality sunk
in as quickly as toes tearing through
sand. There was no escape.

I look at my reflection in the
low tide, late nights. Never allowing
myself to forget. Say it aloud. Repeat
it, again. And again. For clarity.

"He won't change for me."

So, I polarize my thoughts of a
future with you. Rip the cuffs that
once sparkled for you, let it free.
Let it be. Let it be known. I should
have unchained your feet long before
they decided to flee from me. Instead
of decorating your heart with 14kt gold and
being dragged down by dead weight.

Just wait, when you come back
up for air, you'll see how you reach
out in despair. I won't be there, not
even in the vicinity. And see I
miss, the days you were unique
and humble. Cus now you crumble
at any chances of heartfelt happenings.

And look at you now. You get off on the
thoughts of women loving you. You take
pride in the different ways I kiss you. I am
vulnerable. Flesh toned and naked awaiting
your approval. And after you left, I was bare.
I was, knee deep in rusted apologies and
broken promises. And I see how you think
you're untouchable. And I can't un-love it all.

And I touched too close, and now
I don't even want you.

Danielle's first poem.

I wrote my first poem in second grade
I appropriately named it,
"What is Love"

Little did I know it wasn't a
prophetic proclamation of
things discovered but
a plea for things left
unknown and
forgotten

empty.

This is what empty sounds like ...

Do you hear that?
That sadness in the
silence of my soliloquy.
It's deafening. It's damaging.
Quite dreadful, if you really listen.

Let your ears be intentional
and catch the sounds in the
depths of the exhales.

Can you hear the tiredness
in the trusses of my chest?
How in each wave of inhales
and exhales, as I am gaining
new breath, I sound like loss.

Can you hear the wheezes
trying to scratch their way out
of a throat that is far too
exhausted to describe what
love once felt like?

You can't, can you?
All the while, I am left to
wallow in the obscurity of
what would have been and

willingly weep in vacated
chest cavities, awaiting the
resolution of sonority.

And that is the sound I spend
seasons searching for

And that, that is the sound
of empty.

time's up.

I am
so tired
of loving
men who
do not
love me.

I am
so tired
of chasing
dreams in the
darkness and
waking up
in the dead
of day to
nightmares.

I am
so tired
of tripping
over tyrants
and hoping
the next stumble
will bear bruises
of mutual selection.

I am
far too
tired for

fake smiles
and words
that no longer
hold weight.

And I will
wait no more.

things that happen at 2am.

Close your eyes. Cry. Breathe. Cry. Cry. Think about everything you can until the exhale. Cry. Breathe. Shuffle through the covers like you've lost something. Cry. Cry. Cry. Don't forget to breathe. Open your eyes. Stare at the ceiling. Try to make out how the speckles look like constellations. Cry. Struggle to breathe. Pant. Pant. Gasp for air. Breathe. Breathe. Find yourself in the panic. Cry. Sleep. Wake up with the sun. Cry. Tell no one.

what does the night whisper?

Have you ever listened to the
wrestling of words when you
proclaim your love to the night?

strength.

You were filled
with so much pain,
yet still smiled bigger
and brighter than anyone
I had ever known.

fingerprints.

There are dirty
fingerprints on
the foothold
of my soul.

There are traces
of you terrorizing
the finishing's
of my mold.

There are empty pits
partitioning rights over
places that do not
belong to them.

And I am trying
to shake from it,
to not break from it,
but there are these
memories metastasizing,
making it impossible
for me to be
relinquished
from you.

sounds that induce tears:

dial tones
the voicemail forwarding lady
covers shifting during sleepless nights
petty words said in fights
the absence of light
the chill of the darkness
the smell of you left on my pillow
the recitation of unfinished poems at 3am

break through.

When my pen takes
its rightful place
on the page. I pray
that will be enough.

When my words take
the form of courage and
are performed from parched
lips to uninhibited ears

When my sounds slow
and I bear all my burdens
in a book full of poems
I can finally say I have
given birth to
breakthrough.

getting to know my mother.

At jump, we were forced to stop
the swing set conversations about
the way the clouds shaped the sky,

about how the sunset came,
almost as quickly as
tomorrow's thought of
knowing you.

We were so new to each other,

we never, truly knew each other.

We had no idea how hard we
would fall from each other.

And I still hope one day I'll
get to know what that glimmer
of sadness means.

I still hope one day you'll
get to know mine too.

strangers and thieves.

You don't even know me,

yet you talk like
you got what I need.

You don't even know me,

yet you supersede all the others,
you're undercover with your
conquests of me and
you have won me over
all the while.

I have chosen to section my smile away.
To keep close tabs on feelings and emotions that are not
meant to be shared with the likes of people like you.

you cannot treat me like this.

I can already hear your
thoughts plotting against
my smile.

I can already hear mine
fighting to stay sane.

I yell as no one listens -
You, cannot, treat me like this.

You cannot treat me like
screens sifting through
dirt to find diamonds.

You shake me up,
get me dirty and
desolate. Desperate.
Searching
Searching,
searching

she's in there
somewhere,

but spit on me
like grain,

like you've lost the
luxury in my eyes

like the cheap stuff,
not the real stuff.

I don't sparkle
like I did when you
first found me, so make
me feel shame.

And like a fool, I still
replay that first time
you looked at me like the
glittering glaze of jewels,
collecting from the corners
of my smile, lingering and
multiplying like kaleidoscopes.

But now, I see that hesitation
in how you hold me in your eyes;

She doesn't look like the
woman I want her to be.

You once reveled me
a queen, now you're mean

and can't seem to believe
in the woman I am becoming

and entrap me in
ideas you thought up for me.

Sometimes at the end of my day
I fear that it is the end of my days

And I don't know which direction
onward is

you keep taking what isn't yours.

Section off
another territory
in my heart.

Give it away
with a smile
and a promise
to never
let go.

Take some
more.

Drain me
down to my
core. Then tell
me I'm not the
same girl you met
when we were
seventeen, then
leave me.

wishing well.

I wish I could reach
back in time.

Wish I could send
a warned whisper
to myself,

I'd say:

Don't let the entrance of
his touch taint you.

I wish I could take back the
intertwining of our hands,
or the late summer walks where
we gazed into bottomless
stars and spoke of the possibility
loving each other.

And now, I can no longer
fathom the beauty of
a first kiss.

And now, because of you,
I can never truly feel
cleansed.

therapy.

The first time
I went to
therapy
I lied

The second time
I blamed it all
on you

fool that I am.

I repeat the chorus of
pain and disappointment and
love and you and sing it
to myself as punishment.

I should have known better
        …that was the bridge.

The first verse hopes that
you had been more gentle
in your ascension of knowing
my touch,

knows that it must have
been too much a task for you.

Verse two reveals how
we got too caught up in the
starlight of sentences
spoken in the dead
of night.

Exposes how I shared
far too many of my dreams
with you only to wake up alone
that Thursday morning.

And I guess we never
truly saw eye to eye.
Only eyes to lips pursed

and pleading for a
love that was mutual,
fruitful, you know,
something beautiful.

In time, you saw your way
out of all of the doors
you had to pry open
from me. Left them, open
and without protection.

You played the part well,
I must admit. I could see
the sincerity in the way you
moved with me.

In the way you
moved without me.

And what a fool that I am,
for believing in the fear
of falling.

I should have feared
the hands that promised
to catch me.

fake holidays.

Today is national kiss day.
So, I kiss the insides of
me that haven't seen
comfort, and commemorate
the love lost with tight grips,
and tainted glimpses of days
where I could sit and
marvel at the sight of your
lips. Then, remember that
those are the very weapons
that imprisoned me in the
first place.

color blind.

I colored me
different
in years of
tinted tears.

I used
ill-conceived
colors in a mind
that feeds pain with
poems in an attempt
to never feel again.

Hold me in baby blue,
my favorite of colors,
I whisper in the night
as no one listens.

When words aren't enough,
arms become hinge-locked
around knees and buttocks
rocks bare bed frames, and
mattresses just become
unnecessary protection for
pain that is inevitable.

I stop seeing things
and people and pretending
deceit is dirty and live
through the colors
hoping that will get me by

conversations with myself.

I am good enough
I am good enough
I am good enough
I am good enough
until I am not good
enough for you.

And then what am I?

respecting the dead.

After you left me I was terrified.
I didn't want the moments after you'd
passed to resemble anything less of
your laugh.

I did not want to disrespect
the dead.

I'm glad I had faith.

I have always wondered
what it would feel like to
have someone to have
love for me.

I had almost exhausted the
possibility of such a thing

I was almost sure you
wouldn't show yourself
to me in time.

taotaomona

"people before time"

I imagine calloused hands and
thick thighs, like nana says,
"You got those island thighs girl, aya dai!"
meant for lifting latte stones.

I imagine hair falling to the backs
of ankles, sweeping sand and collecting
the complexity of a people that carved
half-moons with their right hands.

Follow the orbit of your palms
with your hips, listen to the dips
in the waves and sway to the
rhythms of the ocean.

Imagine beautiful bare skin against
lavalavas made of the fiber stalks
of bananas, hear the slapping of
hands to upper thighs and stomping
the arches of your feet to meet the
bones of the people before time.

Think about the Taotaomona, the elders,
the nana's and tata's passed, the ones
who are watching us always.
I imagine they are still dancing
along with us, guiding our gracious

minds to the lessons of our island
telling us, *never stop moving.*

guidance.

Close your eyes and make out the
chiseled features of your great
great grandfather, your nana's tata

Listen to the joy in his
Hafa' dai

Listen to the ghosts

To the taotaomonas

To the Anitis

To the sacred spirits of our island

Imagine the power positioned on the
permission of our ancestors

Know in your heart that their presence is needed
Know in your heart that they are good for you
That they will guide you, to you.

repetition.

I know nothing of suffering,
only that I suffer
too often.

I know nothing of literature or
history, only that lessons
taught by you
repeat.

I lost more than you that day.

My grandmother asked me to play my viola at her funeral.
She also asked that no one wear black
To leave the weeping at the door
To flee from grief and celebrate her life with a luau
I spent the two weeks she gave me to prepare practicing
I arranged on a page the melody of her favorite song,
appropriately titled, *home*
I had never played in front of that much family
I had never needed it to mean so much either
I did not want her to hear my pain echoing from the strings
I wanted her to hear the love
Everyone that was in the room with you in your last
moments said you kept whispering,
I want to go home now
You were tired
And we held onto your last laugh until your
cheeks caved in
and after I played my last note, so did my faith in things
good.

Listen to the sounds of
music fill the room.
Let it fill you too.

Listen to the mistakes, the
heartbreak the give and
take of exchanging
looks with love.

Listen to the souls of sirens.
Listen to the pain, to the
hurt in their hearts
when they belt
your name.

Listen and see
if you ever feel
the same.

wasted paper.

I keep journals filled
with metaphors about
loving you.

I have sentences of
similes about how you
are like caves.

I hear the echo
for days and the
sound of your exit
never ceases to
linger.

royalty.

When disappointment
decides to grace my frown,
I wear it like a crown. Let it
glitter and shine for all to
see. I let people awe at the
lies I've created in this
regal display of wealth,
of sovereignty. But never
let powers shift
against me.

take backs.

This is the longest I have been happy in a while

But it's been three weeks since I've smiled
and I'm becoming more and more afraid
that those days are over

I replay the things that bring me joy
over and over
and am stuck on that image of myself
where I'm looking at myself and see
someone else
and I can't help but scream out
for help in the room of my
mind where I know no one will
find me

selfish.

I have spent twenty-four
years weeping for you.

Each year that passes, I tell
myself that loving you is too
tiresome and try to understand
how it is that time and time again
you to loving yourself
over us validate

lost time.

this is the second time
I have chosen to forget

the second pair of hands
that did not seek my
permission

the second time I sold
my soul for silence in a
vessel desperately
in need of careful
handling

the second time where
the escaping of my sanity
was measured
in seconds

I am looking at myself
in the mirror and it
doesn't look like
me anymore.

I am finding
my features falling
at the crevice of
my smile.

I am finding the
imprint of your stench
glass-stained on my
skin and it's not
shining pretty like
it used to anymore.

naïveté

Sometimes I wonder
if you'd notice the
emptiness in my
smile where
happiness used
to reside

Or realize that
blemish in my
eyes came from the
thought of having
loved you

That you'd
check in on me;
the woman
you chose to forget

Who broke her back
in wasted promises
and unhinged futures
and unwound diaries
of entries marked
June 9th, of every look
on your face that
resembled love only
to mock its very existence.
I shouldn't be so stupid.

I will never be the kind of poet that professes their love of flowers. I have much more real things to write about. I have trauma. I have battle scars still bleeding. I know things about people that keep me up at night. I have other people's wars to still fight. I have all of these things. Horrible, horrible things. Yet still make it my mission to write it beautifully.

fallen.

I fell in love with fear.
And now, I fall without
looking. I stitch the
perimeter of my exterior
with my heart. Outline it
in red for dramatic effect.

Leave the sleeves for
celebrations of days where
I am left whole. Barely,
am I holding on. But the
thrill keeps me breathing.
Keeps my heart beating and
the possibility of love does
not turn me away.

I invite this pain willingly.
Will it to the forefront,
stunt growth and replace it
for shortcomings. I laugh
and welcome the excitement
of men ruining me because
at least I can say I am feeling.

the break-up box.

Give me back my shit.
Return all of the over
turned lips that laughed
for you. Give me back
my words of affirmation,
my adoration for you
and forget what
it ever felt like
to be loved by me.

some people's stories change you;

At the funeral everyone
kept telling me you had
something to explain to me

I thought the tears were
self-explanatory

I did not know that
a part of her died
long before I got to
know her smile.

I did not know
she had been
broken all the while.

It took you a month to tell me.

To look me in the eyes
and tell me things you
only heard about in
movies.

When you finished speaking
You gave me this look.

And I was never the same.

squatters.

I do not trust
certain men in
empty houses,

do not
present them
with any more
chances to
squat in homes
that were not built
for them.

I choose Him.

Please,

Don't ever get it twisted
I do not need anyone but
God.

So, when you shift your weight
sitting on that high ass horse
of yours, remember that the
definition and detail of my smile
is because I choose to revel in the
miracles of prayer and thank God
daily for the blessings he has
delivered in the image of your touch

Don't ever get it twisted

There will always be more prayers

There will always be more hands

in the summertime we can be careless.

it seems
as though I've
welcomed
this pain

welcomed legs
and skin that
scream for second
chances

and meet
every night with
tight skirts
and lipstick
that is far too
assertive
to ask for
new names

and men that
turn into
things not
remembered
when I wash my
makeup off the
next morning

questions for the dead

Do you see all that
I'm doing from up there?

Is it clear that I am living
to honor you?

Is it okay that I replicate
your laugh through my poetry?

I think you forgot about me over there.
And I am choosing to blame the distance,
your reasoning for keeping me at a distance,
because the thought of your love lessening
is not another lesson I wish to learn.

things I will not accept.

There are far
too many excuses
I could use to
explain why I
cannot be healed.

There are people
who would label
you a menace.

There are no
more places for me
to kneel and
seek penance.

There are those
who will want
to add to
the wreckage.

Who will think
I expect this

Who will say,
accept this.

It has been a long time
since someone has tried
to know me

It has been a long time
since kisses were laid on
scars and given time to grow

Since promises were
made and kept

It has been a long time since
I've slept and not dreamt and
not cried

Two ways to mourn.

There was so much sadness in losing you

There was also immense happiness

#3

One word drapes the
inside of my right wrist like
an anecdotal anxiety killer.

It's cursive,
it curves and connects to
the language that carries my culture.

It reads, *hagong*

/ ha - gung /

To breathe.

This was the first tattoo I chose to make visible
The first I chose to use as a
capstone of knowing myself.

I repeat it in crisis.

Hagong

/ ha - gung /

To breathe.

Inhale all of your frustrations.
All of the things you feel
consume you.

All of the ways you feel
tainted. Broken.
Damaged.

Inhale all of the anxiety and panic
and exhale, peace of mind.

Breathe. Deeply.

Never let the weight of the world
drag you backwards, be light
and easy, and effortless like
the air that fills your lungs

Breathe.

Be still.

Stop panicking. Stop pacing. Stop
participating in the destruction of your
smile. Stop pretending that everything is okay.
Stop pinpointing every flaw.
Stop picking yourself apart.
Start putting yourself back together.

Breathe.

Let go of the hurt.

Breathe.

Breathe.

Inhale…
…exhale.

Forget all your troubles. Forget
all your struggles. Forget all of
the reasons you want to give up.
Forget people and places that
haunt you. That only stuck by you to
flaunt you. Forget everything that isn't
worth a second
breath.

Breathe.

You will be okay.
You will find a way.
You, will get there.
Just, breathe.

small moments.

 Find me in the small moments.
In between my hand retreating
from the nape of your neck,
when I'm done cradling the kept
chaos of kissing you.

Seconds before the look of
admiration adorned on my eyes,
before it sweeps up from lips, to
blushed cheeks, to the awkward silence
of wanting to find your eyes
waiting for me.

Save time for the off times. When
I've stopped finding the light in
you. When I can't seem to find the
right in you. When I fight with you.
Make up for all the times they let me
down and pick up my insecurities
and cast them away with my worry.

Don't worry, I'll always smile for you.
So long as you hold me in the
tears that have yet to form, and
promise to always offer shelter in
shapes of collarbones. Cling to me
and fill me whole. But still come and
find me in the hazy in-betweens.
I have been broken for a while. But I try
my hardest to still sparkle new for you.

And I try my hardest to catch you right
before sarcasm meets sincerity, in that
moment when you're really there with me.
In those small moments. In the breezes that
leave my face after you've pushed a mountain
of my hair back in its place, right after I look
away in vigil vulnerability. These moments.
Moments before I decide if I'm going to
look away in embarrassment for not being
everything you need or whether or not
I will smile for you.

Will I decided to be without your touch
in moments that I've spent a lifetime
wishing for. If only for a second.
In those seconds, where your eyes tell
me I'm worth everything. Where you're
everything. Where silence fills our lips
to the brim and, on a whim, we invite
the possibility of making every moment
a fairytale. And every moment where
I'm not kissing you feels small.

shadow dance.

Come, shadow dance in the
corners of my smile. Two-step
your way to the old ways of
loving me, sincere and sure of
everything but where you'll find
yourself tomorrow.

Save that thought for
later. Savor, the flavors of love
and dance along the confines of
consciousness with me.

spoken word.

I'm proud of myself
for this growth I've
gathered in the
shape of poetry.

Happy that I no longer
allow anything things that do
not contribute to my smile,
to haunt me.

And that I can recite my
deepest fears in the ears
of strangers and collect
applause where I once
kept insecurities.

star gazing.

I want to be everything you've
talked me up to be. I want to help
find our dreams in the constellations.
To stargaze, in your eyes. Find the
truth in the outlines of your retinas.
Really connect the dots in the webs of
love lost and find the man underneath
the rubble. Recompose our tragedies
and find the shooting stars in the dead
of the night where others were too
near sighted and negligent to point out.

I want to lie, side by side in the grass,
looking up to the sky and tell stories
of gods and goddesses. Imagining ourselves
as creators of love. Commandeering our past
lives and taking seize of our subtle secrets
of a future with one another.

I want to be of the sky. To orbit around
your insecurities and your worries and
allow gravity to hold them like hands
cupping bashful cheeks that smile
slightly after the words, I love you,
are finally brought to light.

I want to be your first wish.

I want you to find me in the depths
of my mangled mind and see the

glimmer in me. I want you to realize
that stars are alive for thousands of
years before they are ever found by
wandering eyes. Look up in the sky
and find me ready for the fall,
I'll make sure to shoot for you.

certainty.

There is not a doubt in my mind that thinks
a day will pass without the welcoming
of your laugh transitioning thought my ears.

for my sisters.

I never truly knew what it meant
to be a part of something until I
met you.

I never truly knew family
that was not my own until
it was draped in your dedication

I never truly knew how
colors would catch
and hold me

I never truly knew how
it would mold me

And today,
I am better because of it

because of you.

redemption day.

There will come a day
when I will no longer cringe
at the thought of loving you.

When your laugh will offer comfort
unparalleled, rare, conscious, and
courteous comfort.

And when your laugh lines retract
and fall back into place, maybe
for once I will not forsake your
beautiful bashfulness for neglect.

And when it is cold and
the men of my pasts retreat to
their corners of deceit you will cling
to me and never let me go

You will cover my shivers, shelter
them in the hinges of your arms
open them and close them
open me and close me.

a meeting of importance.

meet me in the
back and I'll bear
my soul to you,

lay all my shit
bare until I have
nothing else to
share

just promise not
to release my gaze,
not for a second,

don't ever second guess
my love.

fairy tales.

I've never heard of a
love story that was perfect.
Only people, whose eyes
couldn't go two minutes
without singing for each other.

Who couldn't not laugh and
who wouldn't walk without
the soles of their feet in the
same line of syncopation.

Who wake up, side by side
and wink happiness into the
breathes of each other.

And it's never instant, never
simplistic. Its' messy and
sexy. Testy. But it's yours.

the old me.

I am at odds with the
woman I am becoming
I am trying to let go of
everything that no longer
suits me. Of everything
that I used to be.

Love has taught me two things. That in one moment
I can hurt, without warning or boundaries or band-aids.
Without care of casualties or scars, like open bars. That my
pain is an alcoholic reaching for refill and another excuse.

In the second moment, I've learned to look up.
To look past my bruises and doubt and know that love is
sweet and docile. That it is tender. Honest. Caring.
Handsome. That it is waking up in the early morning when
the sun hasn't fully risen and shifting body weight to find
my hand and never letting go even if it means
compromising comfort. That comfort lies in the eyes that
stare back and allow you to love for the second time.

dreams about my grandparents.

I had a dream I was you last night.

I was standing at the red clay wall
that lined the top of the hill separating
your home from all the others.

I walked down to the beach and felt the
sand carry on the hinges of my toes.

I felt the sharpness of the rocks and
shells and things left abandoned.

I closed my eyes and took moment
to live in your moments –

I did not realize you had been living
with your eyes scarred shut until I felt the
coldness of the gun placed to my temples,

It did not shake like I did, it was not
fearful like I was.

I was still and insistent.

I felt his eyes piercing threats so
loud, words were not needed.

I felt the children breathing in the bedrooms,
breeze from the ocean wandering from the
living room window, felt the whistling of

thoughts collecting at the peak of my forehead.

I felt the intensity of two people,
one threatening life, the other,
pleading for it in the silence and
tried not to be suffocated by it.

I felt the pain situated on my heart like
a dumbbell.

Felt the weight of the world on my chest and
years of nights where rest did not come for me.

I felt faith wavering on the last of my rosary beads.

When I woke and returned to myself I wept
for the horrors that had haunted you in your daytimes.

I felt despair.

I felt the exact moment you broke,
and carried that feeling with me like armor.

flight.

I think I'll fall for you

Hold on, let me stretch
my legs, check my pulse
and risk it all for you

Your hands are strong
and caring. Your eyes
are daring. And I've been
carefully cradling the
truths you've bestowed on me.

Can you feel it in your
chest like I do?

Think about the wind
brazing your bones

About the rollercoaster
ride we've crafted ourselves

The screams and smiles
too big to be contained
on the outlines of our faces

New feelings and new places

Think about fear and flight
and frills and fantasy

and faith and fate
and me

I hope the fall sets us free

waste.

Every day I sit here,
writing poetry about how
constellations form at the
peak of your forehead,
of how you laid knowledge
on my unmade bed,
and let me cuddle in the
thought of you,

and stare at blank pages
and empty words
and stars that I wasted
so many wishes on.

*As a writer, I am complacent. I let silence fill in days
where I am content in my life. And when the day comes where
unknown fear arises, my fingers take to the pen and fill pages of all of
the ways I will be broken when you are gone.*

three poems working against the curve of my smile.

1. You get up
and walk
towards the
hallways I've
closed off
from you,

to the rooms
and beds and
heads I've
decided were
no longer meant
for occupying.

I don't tell you
to follow me,
but you do

I don't tell you
I want your
hands to grip
my hips either

2. At this
point, I am
done sifting

through the
notion of
love or lust

or zippers or,
abstention.

At this
point, I am
filled to the
brim with
sadness,

with men
who feel
it is their
duty to fill
me, even if
I never asked
them to.

3. You never
stopped to see
if it made me smile
like it used to.

It didn't.

I pray for you at night.
Pray that your burdens don't
become you.

That God will provide you with the
strength to find your way to yourself
and sometimes,
back to me.

we fall down.

Get up.

Get, up.

Don't ever let him see you cry.

Don't ever let him know
these poems are about him.

Don't give him any more power
than the electric shocks he's
propelled from your smile.

I think he's still living a
lie off that power.

I think he's still chasing your
skies with the hours of
images you mapped out
for him in metaphor.

Like the ones about the clouds
about the crowding of love
about the fluff,

all the stuff trapped in your head
that you condensed and allowed
to evaporate into his arms.

You told him you watched the
clouds when no one was looking.

You told him your dreams lived
up there - that you'd die before ever
being brought back down by the rain,
that you had spent years
fighting the pain.

And here you are, barely sane
barely making time to pick
yourself up in the morning
to see if the rain stopped.

You assume the downpour
becomes hail

You assume that when you
muster up the strength to
stand you'll fail,
you'll flail.

But the truth is,

we all fall down
every once and awhile.

The real test is in smiling
through bruised tail bones and
poems about men who are
no longer relevant.

So, get up.

Live a new day, a new way
and thank whatever God you know
in those clouds that the fear of failure
is no longer an issue.

truth is,

I am blessed
to have ever
known this
amount of
pain.

I think,
it makes me
stronger.

My family is a setting sun. We carry each other in our palms. Shape our smiles in the image of the crescents. Raising each other up the best we can. When it is our turn to wane and wonder about the things that haunt us, we wait with the tide. With the absence of light.
With the welcoming of the moon.

We are getting tired. We are alternating between sun and sand and hoping one day we can all know what it feels to be on leveled ground again.

muscle memory.

I close my eyes and
touch my hands to
remember how the
curve of your palms
felt inside mine.

I recall every crinkle,
every twist and turn
mapped out in the shape
of M's and pray I never
have remember the
pinprick draft of your
hand leaving the small
of my back again.

consumption.

love will knock the shit out of you sometimes
love will bear bruises and contusions
love will fly you right off the handle
will share truths with you that you might not
be strong enough to handle
it will be your downfall
have you question it all
it will test you
take the best of you
love will fill you with joy
fill all of your voids.

I have always been the person that finds a way.
I have never downplayed daydreams. Only spent nighttime's
and lifetimes making sure they
don't do anything other than
come true.

I can't love you yet.

You don't seem to see the
shadows hiding in the curve
of my laugh lines, or the doubt
that follows the release of my
tongue when I'm speaking
of you.

don't let them sleep on you.

You are unexpected.

You are long awaited.

You were left alone to fester
and blossom and topple
over things that no long suit
new ages of thinking.

You, are growth.

Sometimes,
I swear, it's like your
moons are in sync with the
soft swells of my back,

curving, to the soft
burrow of your
fingertips.

As I sit in front of you,
I am trying to escape the
sun as it catches the look of
dejection on my face,

the sun is bright, but,

not as bright as my smile,
you told me that.

You told me, I was so
special to you.

And though I remember
the second guess of your
hand on my cheek
I had no idea that in the
in the morning you'd be gone.

civil war.

I am overworked and run
down, with quarter sized
calluses stamped on the
insides of my palms.

My chest hurts, and
it feels like a boulder
has taken refuge on
my lungs, and I'm wheezing,
frantically, and still
freaking out from last Friday
when I was left all alone to
face the voices in my head
the ones that come
with the pit black siege
of the night sky.

I sit, cradled like a
child pleading for
redemption, I am pleading
for pastime. I am panting,
in and out, in and out. Pacing,
in circles, going nowhere and
everywhere at the same time.
Crying, for what seems like an
eternity, and even though it
is over in fifteen minutes time I

am terrified of its return, and of
days that never seem to end.

And in the morning
I wake, same as every day, with
eyes wide as rivers and hands,
still shaking but placed by my
side, instead of wrapped around my
five-foot two frame in a frantic panic
and I go on like nothing has changed me.

we were no good for each other.

We were exhausted
at the lives we have
dreamed up for ourselves.

We lost concept of reality.

We never told anyone how it
hurt to not be holding one another.

We never told each other how it
hurt even more to stay.

I count your absence in seconds.

There are 480 miles between the last
place I kissed you.

And my heart beats a mile a
minute thinking about all of
the times I should have said
I love you
    but didn't

They say that distance makes
the heart grow fonder

but I was already fond of your chest hinged
under my chin the mornings we got to
wake up with each other

And now every other sunrise, I wake and
am not greeted by the fluttering of your eyes
I take time to count the miles between us
in the speckles of my sheets.

And now,
it seems that
days turn into
nights that make
lifetimes of overworked
laugh lines traced in
the image of you
holding me.

we'll never know.

I stare for hours,
wondering if I'll
ever be good enough
for people like you.

And I swallow all
of the words I should
have never allowed to
escape my tongue
in the first place.

Make me feel special,
then leave me. Repeat
this until I am too tired
to notice a change in
fake smiles.

Until my cheeks have
caught up with my
tears and my fears
take over.

Until I'm left,
lost, and confused
because I thought
it would be right this
time.

I could have loved you,
if you let me.

I guess now
we'll never know.

the reckoning.

We want fires that burn. Poems that hurt. Words that are so painstakingly blunt they break barriers. People that are so honest it brings others to their knees.

Eventually, they will beg and they will plead. *"Please end your statement with a period and not a dagger."*

They will cry. They will deny all your claims. But push through and let blood flow. If you don't write it, nobody will. And then you'll be subjected to anybody's will. And we don't have time for that shit. We don't have time to sit. We are in a revolution. So, use your words precisely.

We want fires so big your bigotry dissipates. We want poems that hurt. We want words so painstakingly blunt they break barriers. People that are carriers of the truth.

People that dispute. People that bring you to your knees. Beg for forgiveness. Plead for people who placate. Who pacify. Who fear the fire. Go with them. The Begging and the pleading. And show them that you are the force to be reckoned with.

leave your shame at the door

*lay your troubles on the floor and
stand in front of the one who's name
begins and ends with*

victory.

if need be.

You were so endearing like
sunflowers in the summertime.

Your stalks were never anything
less than valiant.

You were both stout and
amiable; with hues of yellow and
orange,

Your core was nourishment, meant to
feed the world, if need be.

Your pedals peeled back, one by
one, and each day you gave your all,
only to be picked apart
all over again.

falling in love with an artist.

It is the way you follow your art.

The way you hold your
heart, the way you hold verse at
the tip of your tongue and
reveal prophecy.

repetition.

I love
and love
and love
and cry
and feel
everything,
but loved.

I break
like houses
made of glass
and
wish the
squatters
would be
more kind
to my architect
when opening
and closing
doors that
were never
meant to be
occupied.

I cry
and cry
and cry
and search
for rooms

that can store
my baggage and
sadness
and wake up
to a cold bed
wanting to love
again.

As I age, I find myself
looking more and more like
my mother.

And I know with time,
I will begin to see you in the
pieces of my smile that broke
when you left us.

I know we will meet again.

this is me being forward.

I have not always been the kind of person that was still standing in my acquisitions of love. I have often found myself faltering at the idea of feelings. Often question the reason for the setting of the sun. I never thought I'd be the one to find the one. I never thought I'd meet you. Or rather, be re-introduced to the idea of your hand brushed against my cheek. And I tried to sneak and peek and awe at the transitioning of our eyes against the opposing skin. I crafted stories in my head about a love that would, finally win. I wrote stories and poems and memory books, scribbled them on the insides of my eyelids and sat back and meditated on the fairytale endings of a love with you. I let the lending hand you politely placed on my heart heal me and steal away any image of a man that was anyone but you.

I sometimes feel that I even tried not to love you. I think I knew how I'd fall for you. Think I knew that there would be a day where I thought about every second that passed without the entrance of your voice calling me name. That I would cringe at every moment where I wasn't replaying your last half spoken word or sarcastic joke like my favorite song. I knew it wouldn't be long, until your charm wore me down. I knew I wouldn't be able to tell up from down and that direction would eventually be obsolete because any way with you is movement forward.

things.

love
heartbeats
lilac colored nail polish
hair ties for when my
hair gets too thick
and the band finally
pops
bad days
good days
blue skies
blankets for days where
all we want to do is
lay until the dark comes
and choose another path
to embark on
city visits
agendas hidden
friends
sisters
empty notebooks
pens slowly running out
of ink, be quick in your
writings
waiting on the rain
and a struggle that
just gets too hard to bear
emotions that rage

pages that tear from

fear
the mere thought
of losing something that means
so much
the idea
that the little things
just might be able to
bring you faith

truth.

As I began to speak,
my voice vibrated like
the disposition of
blues music. My tone
was sad, I looked to the
ground to avoid everyone's
eyes. I cried, and felt hands
on my shoulder, felt eyes
on me, the understanding kind.

At that moment,
it was no longer difficult to
spill my truths

At that moment,
I saw a room full of
women ready to pour
love into chest cavities
that had since been
emptied from doubt.

gps.

Let my skin
be your map. Trace
my stretch marks
and my pain. Feel
my hips and
the dips and
valleys of my
stride. Strong and
questioning. Question
the motives of my lips.
Plump. Soft. Read
the stories my breasts
tell with their weight.
There's gravity in
every crevice you just
have to wait.

Be patient with my
ten fingers and
ten toes. Maybe
they'll lead me to you,
after you've spent
enough time,
searching for me.

Watch as my melanin
fluctuates from pale
cinnamon to bitter
butterscotch and know
that every flavor of me

is more intriguing
than the last.

Hold my thighs in your
palms and know that
they are closed gates,
shaped in the image of
guardians. Let them
guide you to my
temples. Focus
on my mind.

Stare at it.
And understand
that one day,
I'll let you inside.

when thoughts form.

It is okay to keep the secrets that live inside your smile until they are ready to pass your lips.

if only for a little while.

When it storms,
I like staring out of the
window. Watching, raindrops
hit the ground, like syncopated
rhythms, offbeat and irregular,
sporadic yet sweet, inconsistent
yet sincere.

I listen as the
dispositions of the droplets
fall with the same sense of
confusion that sparks my
fear, and I'm sad— and I
sit, and hope that the morning
will bring better breezes. That
the breath of the sky is new
and promising, like you were.

You, were soft and
sudden like shooting
stars that people search
for when no one is looking,
soothing yet electric, like
your heartbeat. The gulps of
rain hit the glass, steady and
endearing and right on time.

Like the rain and the stars, you
came with the new day. When
the uninterrupted dew

146

was still a mystery.

When the sun in the
mornings barricade
the rain, if only for a
little bit. You whispered
soft fallacies into my
light-heartened temples
and me, naïve and willing,
I soaked up your knowledge
and had never been more
ready to accept you.

And for a while, I felt,
unburdened, and didn't
sit up all night wondering
about the clouds that
never seemed to clear, and
I didn't have to live in fear.

If only for a little while,
I was happy.

cash machine.

Cash out
the thoughts of
touching me.

Count it's
worth,

Know it's
valued.

Know,
I value you.

for you.

I want to write something beautiful for you. I want to tell you how I wake up unafraid of your hands against my face. That I've measured their gentleness and labeled them harmless. That I do not wish against the pattern of your footsteps because I know they are reciprocal, and residual, and risking everything to make it back to me each time they walk away. I want you to know I've memorized your pace. And your face. Rewired my brain to know when you're on your way to kissing me. I love when you kiss me. And I want you to know that too. It's important. It's simple. It wins wars. It's endured winters of blisters and when I met you in the summertime it was ready to find me. Our last kiss lasted three seconds. I do not have any alliterations or anomalies for that fact. But I have been replaying it over and over and replicating it in my daydreams of you. In today's dream, you grazed my knee with your pinky finger. And like a schoolgirl I took those two seconds where you touched me, and imagined two decades of your fingers on my skin. It was beautiful. This. Us. What was matters no more than the dew on fresh grass in the morning, it fades. Goes away. Is made for new feet to graze its blades and make paths in the green back to me. I want to tell you that you are new days. Dew paved sun rays rested on cheeks washed clean from the way, you say, *baby.*

when you are alone with the night;

Have you ever listened to
the wrestling of words
when you proclaim your
love to the night?

here is a moment of honesty:

You broke me.

And I am trying
desperately
to pick up the
debris before
it's wiped clean.

I am trying to
make things
look better than
what they
truly seem.

I'll be honest,
I never knew
just how effortless
you'd make your escape
from my arms.

I'm half
impressed,
half left in
distress because
I adorned you as
my safehouse.

And I'll be honest,
on your account,
I never expected

to reflect on a love
in one poem and
write of the obliteration
of affection in the next.

tao tao tano
the people of the land.

These are the people who stand
between your egos and our culture.
The people of Guam.
I am halfway across the world
and weep for them. I am half
of their worry.

Half of their despair if we
are chosen to be demolished.
I am tired of men claim our lands
for target practice. I am tired of
pissing contests.

I am tired of people who do
not seek to understand.
Tano i' man Chamorro
Know us.

We are not a sarcastic tweet
on diplomacy. We are the sea.
We are the wide hips of America that
were never consulted for dancing.
We are aligning our palms with the
sky. Draping our thighs with motions
to low tides, we are asking God for
forgiveness, though we have
no true fault in the matter.

We are collateral damage.
So, you choose to strip our pride
with missiles and bad grammar, we
will rebuild our lands with latte
stones and prayer.

Tao Tao Tano.
We are the people of Guam.
We will always be here.

* *Tano i' man Chamorro – The land of the people; the land of the Chamorros.*

this is not a poem.

The last time I wrote a poem about loving anyone
it was welcomed with chaos. This is not a poem.
And you are not just anyone.

happy tears.

Whenever I am left with a
moment to sit and think
about how you helped
reconstruct my smile,
I cry.

Not because I am sad,
but because I am so
incredibly happy, my
tears can't help but
overflow.

Columbia, SC.

I often wonder if it is coincidence or
comedy that all the men I've
committed to are from Columbia.

The list is short, I assure you.

And as I sit, and reflect on men
and the love, and the existential threat
of chest cavities being pillaged and
picked apart for glimpses of sincerity,
I remember something I once
read about love in an article
from Cosmopolitan…

Columbia, SC pt. 2

*Cosmo said that in your lifetime,
you will have three great loves or
relationships.*

    1. The love that looks right.

The envy of all.

The quiet nightmares of two people,
first experiencing love. The one that
has nothing to compare itself to so
you're a fool, engulfed in adolescent
shortcomings and love sung behind the
lockers at lunch time.

Don't be fooled. This love is not for us.

It's merely to meet societal expectations.

It's, idealistic love.

Don't let it hold you longer than the
length of your smile.

Don't go miles searching for
validation of love that looks like this one.

    2. The love we wished was right.

The love that is septic and cyclical and
sits at the top of your tongue waiting
for water on wounds he poured salt on.

Each time in love number two you will
expect for a different outcome

Each time you will crawl back, lay in the
insecurities etched in your clasped hands
Each time you will cry

Each time you will glare at a swollen belly
of broken promises and search for
nourishment in his eyes only to find hatred.

This love is laced in narcissism.
Let it go as quickly as you can.

      3. This is, *the love that just feels right.*

The one that is.

Before he walks into your life you are broken,
You have let men damage you and you are
over imagining a life where love is possible.

This love blindsides you.
It comes ready for battle and helps defeat
all of your lingering demons.
It shows you that love is not
coupled with depression

This love…

This third love,
will help heal you in the most
selfless and sacrificial way.

This love is velcro.

It is finding all of the grooves and curves of
your mind and clinging to it wholeheartedly.
It is stuck with you.

This love has no real expectations, it comes
as sudden and unbeknownst as laughter

It is free flowing and so easy you almost
don't know it's there, until you do.

This is the love that shows you
all of the things you left in your hometown

All of the things you tried so desperately to escape

This love, *is fate.*

freedom time.

There are stories that live
under my fingertips,

waiting for pens and paper
and keyboards and laptops
and love to set them free.

long distance sucks.

But when I am with you
I lay my head to your heart
and guide my hand across
your chest.

I trace out a map
of the next fifty years
I'll spend loving you.
I use the dips in your
abdomen to tell me when
we've reached a new
destination, a new stop
in our haven.

A new place where your
eyes will meet mine and
we've got all the time to
forget we're even apart at all.

And when I'm with you
I slip into realms of
"anything is possible"
where we do the impossible
and distance is a concept
we have yet to acknowledge

where the only directions
we need towards each other
is in figuring out where the fall is.

When you choose to remain
consistent in your casting
away of responsibility

I almost feel free

Like I don't have to
pretend or hope for
something that will
never happen.

my throat is on fire.

I have this
secret. This
sentence,
burning
holes on the
insides of my
mouth. Making it
hard to decide
whether to speak
my truths or
swallow them.

in all my years of dreaming,
i never thought i'd have the
pleasure of waking
up to you

never thought i'd find the
soft swell of bearings on your
bottom lip, or, feel the map of
my life laid out on the narrowing
of your rib cage

i never thought my prophetic poems of
loving someone like the sun
would ever be found anywhere but
on the page

and now, i have stopped ending them
with periods and started ending them with
you

I am magic.

I am magic.

I illuminate from
toe nail to
tousled curl.

I radiate silvers
and golds and
hold the mysteries
of poetry on my
tongue.

I am one for the books.

So come read about me.

Come see about me.

Come ruminate in
my pages, find the
glitter in the way
I say, *I love me,*

search for the
prose-y goods, the
ones where I admit

the crown on my
head is laced with
insecurities and the

dust of diamonds,

where I reveal how
heartbreak unraveled
on unrelenting shoulders
and created crowns for
queens like me.

Where I reveal
how I have collected
jewels from the parts
of shattered smile, from
people not kind or
smart enough to
comprehend the kind
of magic they were
disrupting.

Wonder Woman.

I want to be the woman
of your dreams

I want you to see me in
years of daytimes and
sleep with me always
on your mind.

put on your good clothes.

The day I knew I loved you
I felt as though I had secrets
spilling out of the seams
of my chest

The day after that,
I laid my knowledge
on a blank page and
wrote an epitaph for all
of the men who died
in my daytimes after
consistency no longer
suited them

I then, dressed my wounds
in silks and satin and
danced to the place where
our eyes first met

this is what a future looks like.

Today I looked at the
calendar and mapped
out the days to be
spent with one another.

I made plans for us.

because of you. I am changed.

Last night, when I was
sound asleep, sifting through
all of the ways I imagined
you'd say my name, I
held on tightly to the
possibility of never
letting you go.

And today -
today, I woke and
looked at the day like
it had been dressed in
your smile.

And that,
that was real.

That, placed the
touch of Eden
on the shoulders of
Adams trust.

Trust me -
we told this to each other,
and laid naked for
everyone to see what
we meant to each other
You, see me
for all that I am
and I, I am risen from

the lengths of your
Inhales - We inhale
and exhale the way
we imagine, i love you,
sounds on the tips
of our tongues.

And yesterday,
I thought
of only
you.

And as the days pass
I get on my knees
pray, let this last

And marinate
in the minutes and
seconds of days
that begin and
end with you
loving me.

clairvoyance.

You are the
parts of me
that still work.

You are the perks
of letting myself
become art.

You are the start
and finish of blood
flow.

The rapid tingle in my chest.

The difference between
think, and know.

I still get nervous talking to you.

Sometimes I want to ask you things. To tell you things. To share my world with you. But I am the type of person that believes timing is everything. And sometimes, just because I know something, or don't know something, does not mean that it is the right time to spill the secrets scribbled on my palms. Sometimes, I still hide my hands in prideful pockets, searching for all the right words I want to reveal to you.

I remember now.

I used to write poems about
how I would be content with
never knowing love again.

How the feeling of love
was not worth the monumental
melodrama of heartbreak.

But with one touch of your
hand to my cheek, I realized
just how weak minded I was.

In that instant, I was once
again an advocate for love.

labels mean nothing without action.

I once labeled myself
a master of words.

Now I know, it is
not the words that are
so miraculous, but the
ability to define truth.

To lay it out, palms
open, and pulsing and
allow strangers into
it's grasp.

That, is the true
mastery.

Everybody has that one person that is unlike all the others. Everybody has that feeling in their gut. The one that punches Morse code poems of all of the reasons you can never let them go.

Last week, I decided
I no longer had the
energy to mourn over
men that never planned
on loving me.

Last week, I decided
to stop dressing up
deceit in delicate silks
and saturating self-pity
in lace lined sleeves.

Last week, I decided
to let you find me
drowning.

Last week, I decided
to let you took a look
at the battle scars
that had been etched
in my smile.

Today, I decided to
trade in suspicion for
hopefulness and
wrap myself up in
all of the ways you
tell me I'm beautiful
and choose loving you
for weeks to come.

grip.

I am in constant
need of your hands
on my heart.

Of your grip on my
thigh.

Come, squeeze the
possibility of tomorrow
in me.

casket dreams.

Put a sunflower on my casket when my day comes. Write the soft words of prose on the petals, blow em softly to the sky, let someone catch my passed blessings, the ones I found tangled in terror only to unraveled carefully to find later find laced with the outline of loving you.

I have prayed for a love like this.
I have also cried and died
and been reborn again in the
image of your smile.

I have waited a while for
your eyes to land on mine.

I have yielded faith and
time and thanked God
daily for allowing me to
know your touch.

I have finally tasted wealth and
correctly relabeled it love.

I have taken the words
you and I and proclaimed it
forever as us.

independence.

I do not live for others.

I say this out loud to myself

And yet, still do not know
what it means to live for me.

living color.

My love,

know that there is art
bleeding from our fingertips

begging to be sketched into
memories where we are always
laughing.

Here, take my hand
watch as color coded
sentiments drip from palm
to cheek to chest to
every inch where you've ever
touched me.

See how you've touched me.

Know that my skin has been your
canvas and any man that comes
after you will bear witness to
your masterpiece.

Take whatever pieces you love
most with you and don't ever
let my absence do anything
other than lift you.
Store our paint set in your
back pocket and be sure

to let the beauty of us
engulf you every once
and a while.

Make sure to still paint your
smile the way I did.

Make sure you pull out that
picture of man I crafted from
your chest and know that
wealth is always surrounding you.

Understand why I chose to paint you
in mahogany and gold.

And know that while the paint may
fade and temper, you can
always come back to me and be
reminded of the beauty of color.

Imagine if I had kept those past stories on me.
If I decided to not let go of the traumatic endings
that were only ever meant to be
where I began.

learning to breathe again.

I love you

I can say that in one breathe

My second breathe, is always dedicated to
experiencing your smile I've spent nights
obsessing about

The third, exhales all of the worries that pass as
more life is lived without being held in your arms

All of the others, are wrapped in the miles that
separate us

Are spent in the tightness of thoughts
surrounding your name

Are released in relief when your voice finally
rests on my ear, when the fear of forgetting the way the
groove and fill of your hand fits in mine is eradicated by
the return of your love lifted by
tongue and melody.

differences.

Pause,

reflect,

look at the
regret you laid
upon his chest
hoping for
mismanagement.

and remember,

he is not
like the others.

there is art in me.

I was broken
up and repurposed
to reflect the
chaos of water
colors.

There is
art in me.

this is joy.

He looked at me, unwavering
in his disposition of words,
and said, *"that had life."*

That was how he chose to
describe me kissing him.

I thought about other things
that caused me joy, like feet,
sinking in the sands of our
mother's lands. Like mango
trees in grandma's backyard,
catch it before it falls, taste
the sweet fruit, taste the
lips of you. Taste how love
marinates on your tongue.

This is joy.

This is life.

This is us dipped in gold,
wrapped in the finest of silks.

This is wealth

This is yearning for everything
you deserve and more.
Because you are worthy of
all the praise.

Of all of the day's
beginning and ending
in *I love you.*

77780621R00113

Made in the USA
Middletown, DE
25 June 2018